G000167923

101 facts about

The ANIMALS at BRISTOL ZOO

BRISTOL ZOO GARDENS

See it · Sense it · Save it

Julia Barnes

First Stone Publishing

FIRST STONE

Published by First Stone Publishing,
an imprint of Corpus Publishing Limited,
PO Box 8, Lydney, Gloucestershire, GL15 6YD,
United Kingdom.

Design: Sarah Williams
Cover Design: Rosie Peace, Appletree Design

First Published 2005
Text and design © 2005 CORPUS PUBLISHING LIMITED
Photography © 2005 BRISTOL ZOO GARDENS

ALL RIGHTS RESERVED

No part of this publication may be reproduced in any material form, whether by
photocopying, scanning, down-loading onto computer or otherwise without the written
permission of the copyright owners, except in accordance with the Copyright, Designs
and Patents Act 1988. Applications should be addressed in the first instance, in writing,
to the Publisher. Any unauthorised or restricted act in relation to this publication may
result in civil proceedings and/or criminal prosecution.

ISBN 1 904439 34 9

Printed in Hong Kong through Printworks Int. Ltd
0 9 8 7 6 5 4 3 2 1

What is it like living in a tropical rainforest? What goes on beneath the sea? Which animals come out at night to hunt? You can find out the answers to all these questions at Bristol Zoo Gardens.

Situated in the heart of the city, on a 5-hectare site, Bristol Zoo is home to more than 400 different species of animal. Within a few minutes' walk, you can see animals ranging from the magnificent Asiatic lions to the terrifying red-kneed bird-eating spider. Around the lake you will catch sight of exotic monkeys, such as the golden-headed lion tamarin (below), and you can visit the western lowland gorillas on their island home.

Bristol Zoo gives us the chance to see spectacular animals – but it does more than that. It is working to save animals in the wild, as well as breeding endangered animals at the zoo. It is only through these projects that some of the world's most fascinating animals stand a chance of survival.

Asiatic lion has a smaller mane, and it has a roll of skin running along its underbelly.

3 At one time, there were only 100 Asiatic lions left in the wild. Now they are protected and live in the Gir Forest nature reserve in north-west India.

1 We all think of lions coming from Africa, but there is another kind – the Asiatic lion (above) – which lives in India.

2 African lions and Asiatic lions look very similar. Some differences are that the

4 When lions go hunting they take up their favourite positions and then close in on the prey animal with a sudden burst of speed that may reach 58 kmph (36 mph).

5 Western lowland gorillas (below right) cannot swim, and so they are free to roam on their island home. The gorillas' home is specially designed with climbing frames, platforms, ropes and trees, so you can see how a gorilla would behave in the wild.

6 A male gorilla stands 1.8 m (6 ft) tall, and weighs around 195 kg (32 stone). But these are the gentle giants of the animal world, living on a diet of fruit and vegetables.

7 They are among the most intelligent animals that live on the land. A few have even learned hundreds of words in sign language.

8 Destruction of tropical rainforests means that many species of monkeys are dying out in the wild. Breeding programmes in zoos such as Bristol are helping to save rare species from extinction.

9 The golden lion tamarin (above), from Brazil, is one of the rarest rainforest animals, with only about 1,000 left in the wild.

10 The tamarin's natural enemies include eagles, jaguars and snakes, but people destroying their forest home has proved to be a far greater danger.

11 The red-race Javan langur (below left) from Indonesia, gets its name from its bright orange fur. In fact, 20 per cent of the population are black.

12 In the wild, spider monkeys (right) rarely come down to the jungle floor. They swing through the trees, often gripping with their tail so their hands are free to gather food.

13 On the look-out, the spider monkey stands on two feet, using its tail to hang on to a support.

apart from feeding, the mother leaves it to the father and older brothers and sisters to care for her babies.

16 The howler monkey (below right) is the loudest monkey in the world. Its call can be heard up to 4.8 kms (3 miles) away.

14 Geoffroy's marmosets (above) are small squirrel-like monkeys from South America. They live in groups of 8-10 animals.

17 These monkeys live high in the canopy of the rainforest, and use their voices to keep in touch with other members of their group.

15 Females usually give birth to twins but,

18 Squirrel monkeys (right) live in communities of 25-30 animals. The monkeys sleep together, and then they divide into smaller groups to look for food.

19 As soon as a baby squirrel monkey is born, it is carried on its mother's back, clinging on tightly as she climbs through the trees.

20 A bird often uses its bill as a special 'tool' for finding, catching, and eating food.

21 The greater flamingo (below left) stands in the shallow waters of lakes and rivers. It uses its tongue and curved bill to suck in water containing particles of food such as algae and shrimps.

22 It is the colouring in the shrimps that makes flamingos' feathers go pink.

(below), which comes from the rainforests of South America, can find a use for its huge bill which measures up to an amazing 23 cms (9 ins).

23 The pink-backed pelican (above) plunges its head underwater, and fills its huge pouch with fish and water. It then shakes out the water, and swallows the fish whole.

24 It is hard to believe that the toco toucan

25 But the bill gives the toucan a big advantage. It can reach into the thorniest bushes to find the fruit that other birds cannot get to.

26 The little egret (below) stands as still as a statue waiting for a sign of a fish in the water below.

27 Then, with split-second timing, it uses its long, thin bill to seize the fish, which it swallows whole.

28 The kea (above), from New Zealand's South Island, is a master of destruction. It raids rubbish dumps and even attacks sheep, landing on their backs and pecking them with its sharp, curved bill.

29 Intelligent and inquisitive, the kea will rip up anything it comes across. A car hire firm in New Zealand estimates that keas cost them £14,000 a year in damage to their cars.

30 The crowned pigeon (right), from New Guinea, has more beauty than brains. This exotic-looking bird is the largest member of the pigeon family, and is as big as a turkey.

31 Crowned pigeons live on the forest floor, foraging for fruit, seeds and snails. They are so easy to catch that their numbers have fallen as they have been hunted for food and for sport.

32 Nocturnal animals rest during the heat of the day, and come out at night to find food. When you step into Twilight World, it is like going on a night safari.

33 The sand cat (below) prowls though desert sands, hunting for small rodents and reptiles. The pads of its feet are covered with long hair to protect them from the scorching sand.

34 In the dark of night, the sand cat uses its big ears to listen for animals moving about underground, and then digs them out with its front paws.

35 Livingstone's fruit bats (above) spend the day hanging upside down in colonies called 'camps'.

36 They use their big eyes and excellent sense of smell to find fruit and nectar. There are now only about 1,000 of these bats left in the wild.

37 The sugar glider (right), from the Australian rainforests, has perfected the art of gliding.

38 Emerging at night from its nest in the trees, the sugar glider launches itself, spreading out flaps of skin on either side of its body like wings.

39 The sugar glider can 'fly' for up to 50 m (165 ft) before landing on a neighbouring tree.

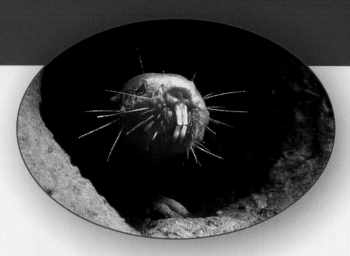

40 The two-toed sloth (below) takes life easy, hanging upside down in the canopy of the South American rainforest.

41 Using claws like hooks, the sloth hangs on to the branches. It eats, sleeps, breeds and feeds its young in this position.

42 Because of the sloth's upside-down life, its hair grows the opposite way to most animals so that the rain can drip off.

43 Naked mole rats (above) spend their entire lives underground, living in colonies of 100 or more animals, and feeding on roots.

44 It is neither hot nor cold underground, so the mole rats do not need fur. They have very poor eyesight, and use their whiskers to guide them through the dark tunnels of their home.

45 Only one female in the colony – the queen – is allowed to breed, and she produces 10-20 pups in each litter.

46 Owl monkeys (right) are the only species of monkey that are active at night. Their large eyes give them excellent night vision.

47 An adult male and female will spend their lives together, living in a small family group of mother, father, and up to four offspring.

48 The animals of Bug World may be small but many of them can pack a punch if they are attacked.

49 A bite from the North American black widow spider can kill a man. It is only the females who bite, and they kill their partners after mating.

50 The red-kneed bird-eating spider from Mexico (left) has big ideas when it comes to food. It lives mostly on other invertebrates, but will also catch small mammals, reptiles and birds.

51 In the zoo they are fed on locusts, crickets and dead mice.

52 The imperial scorpion (above),

from West Africa, lives on the carcasses of dead animals, but it can attack and kill by holding on to its prey with its powerful pincers and ripping its victim apart.

53 The Mombassan train millipede (above), from East Africa, is a peace-loving animal that lives on decaying leaves and fruit.

54 But if it is disturbed, the millipede can emit an irritating liquid from the sides of its long body.

55 The giant violet-winged grasshopper (below) uses surprise as its chief defence. The grasshopper flashes its bright blue wings, confusing the attacker and giving the grasshopper time to escape.

56 What does a snake, a lizard, a crocodile and a tortoise have in common? The answer is, they are all cold-blooded reptiles that need the heat of the sun to become active.

57 The Aldabran giant tortoise (below) weighs up to 250 kg (550 lbs), and can live for more than 100 years.

58 The ancestors of these giant tortoises were probably normal-sized tortoises, but because they had no natural enemies on the Aldabran Islands – and there was plenty of food – they just kept on growing!

59 The rhinoceros iguana (below right) gets its name from the three horny lumps on its snout, which are like miniature versions of rhinoceros horns.

60 After mating, the female lays about 20 eggs in an underground tunnel. After 6 months, the eggs hatch, and the young have to look after themselves – with no help from their parents.

61 The gila monster (above right) from the deserts of south-west America, is one of only two poisonous lizards in the world.

62 If the slow-moving gila monster is attacked, it uses its powerful bite, and the victim's wound fills with poison. Death follows within hours.

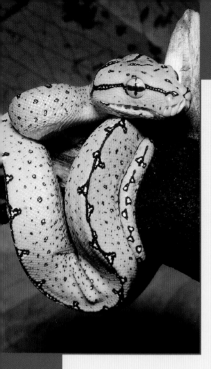

63 Despite their name, green tree pythons are golden-yellow or brick red when they are young (left).

64 It is only when they are adults that they become green to blend in with the leaves of the tropical rainforest.

65 The blue poison arrow frog (right) from the South American rainforests is beautiful but deadly. Poison is secreted through its skin, and even a lick can prove fatal to some animals.

66 The Choco indians pin a frog to the ground with a stick, and wipe their arrows on its skin. The 'poison arrows' are then used for hunting.

68 The female West African dwarf crocodile lays her eggs in a nest of rotting vegetation, which keeps them warm.

69 When the eggs hatch, she carries the young (below) to the water's edge and releases them.

67 The Philippine sailfin lizard (above) lives in trees along river banks in south-east Asia. When it is disturbed, the lizard drops from its branch to the water below, where it swims to safety.

70 Where there is water, there are fish, and in the Aquarium you can discover fish that live in seas, in lakes and rivers, among coral reefs and in mangrove swamps.

71 The giant gourami (below) lives in the still, slow lakes of south-east Asia, where it grows to around 76 cms (2 ft 6 ins) in length. Despite their great size, gouramis are peace-loving vegetarians.

72 Archer fish live in mangrove swamps. When an archer fish spots an insect on an overhanging branch, it shoots a jet of water that knocks the insect into the water.

73 The most colourful fish in the world live around coral reefs. The regal tang (above right) is

(below) has a special coating on its skin that protects it from the stings.

75 The clown fish stays close to the anemone, protected from its enemies. In return it makes short trips to the reef, returning with food that the anemone can share.

one of the 2,000 species that are found in these waters.

74 Most coral reef fish keep away from the sea anemone, as it has thousands of stinging tentacles. But the clown fish

76 Penguins and seals look comical on land, but they are superb underwater swimmers.

77 The South American fur seal (left) can dive to depths of 170 m (558 ft) and, by closing its nostrils, it can stay under water for up to 7 minutes.

78 When a seal is hunting fish, it can reach speeds of up to 40 kmph (25 mph).

79 In 10 seconds a seal can travel 110 m (360 ft) under water, compared to the fastest human swimmer, who could cover only 21 m (69 ft).

80 Penguins are flightless birds. Under water, they 'fly' along using their wings as flippers, cutting through the water at great speed.

81 There are 17 different species of penguin – at Bristol Zoo, you will see African penguins, and gentoo penguins (below and right).

82 Penguins feed only at sea, but they come on to land to breed. They live in big, noisy groups known as rookeries. When the chicks hatch out, one parent stays on land to guard them while the other goes off to find food.

83 North American river otters (below) are one of the most playful of animals. You can see them chasing each other, sliding down banks or playing with stones – just for fun!

84 Otters live on fish and frogs, and underwater they use their stiff whiskers to search for food.

85 The pygmy hippopotamus (top right) is found in swamps and alongside rivers in the tropical rainforests of West Africa.

86 This hippo prefers the single life and marks its personal territory by whirling its small tail to scatter dung.

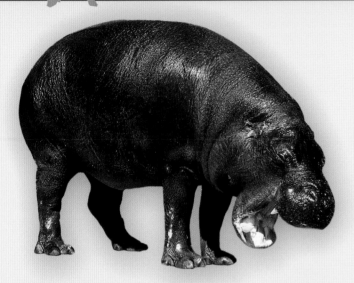

stay under the surface for several minutes, using its nose as a snorkel.

89 Tapirs are ancient animals – they have been on earth for around 55 million years – but they are under threat in the wild.

87 The Brazilian tapir (below right) uses its flexible nose to find plants and roots on the forest floor.

88 When in danger, the tapir takes to the water where it can

90 Black-tailed prairie dogs (below) are not dogs at all – they are actually squirrel-like members of the rodent family.

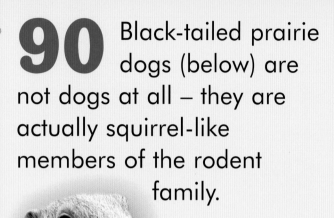

91 Prairie dogs live on the great open grasslands of North America. Their colonies are known as towns.

92 If an eagle soars overhead, threatening to attack, a prairie dog will give a sharp 'bark' to warn others of the danger.

93 Meerkats (above), from the hot, dry

plains of southern Africa, also operate an early warning system to protect them from hunters.

94 While most of the group are on the look-out for insects to eat, one meerkat will be posted as a guard.

95 The okapi (right) is a shy, secretive animal that lives in the dense African rainforest.

96 It was only discovered in the early 20th century,

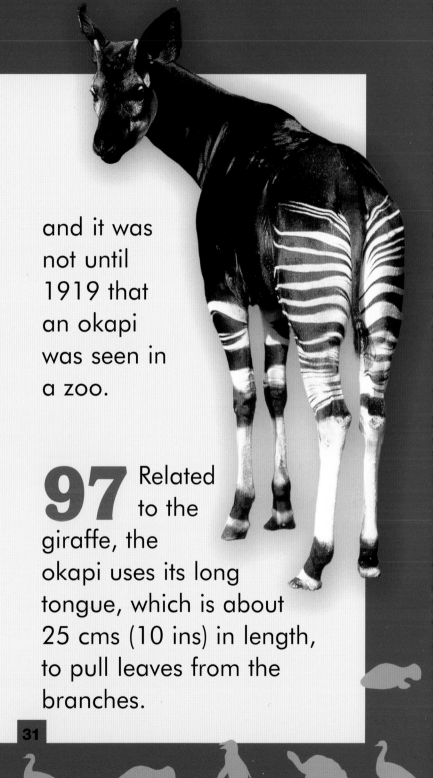

and it was not until 1919 that an okapi was seen in a zoo.

97 Related to the giraffe, the okapi uses its long tongue, which is about 25 cms (10 ins) in length, to pull leaves from the branches.

98 The red panda (below) is also known as the red cat bear.

99 This gentle animal lives in the forests of the Himalayas, where it spends the day sleeping among the trees. At night it goes in search of its favourite food: bamboo shoots.

100 The red panda is in danger of dying out in the wild, but fortunately they are now breeding successfully at Bristol Zoo.

101 We must support zoos such as Bristol, and join the battle to save animals such as the red panda, before it is too late.